Innovation in Services Marketing

(Navigating Services Marketing in a Digitally Connected

World)

DR. SHYAM BANSHIDHAR SHUKLA

ISBN: 9798895884812

DEDICATION

Dedicated to my Parents & my students whom I interacted

directly or indirectly.

TABLE OF CONTENTS

MARKETING OF SERVICES

S

ACKNOWLEDGMENTS

I sincerely acknowledge the support which I got from my students of different batches since 2005. Every stream and every batch has given me lot of inspiration to write this book while teaching and shaping them. My daughter Suyesha and wife Seema has supported me for completion of this book.

1

UNDERSTANDING SERVICES

'The aim of services marketing is to know and understand the customer and not only provide but guarantee the best of services available on Globe.

Introduction to Services

Services are intangible products that cannot be seen, touched, or stored. They involve a transaction where no physical goods are

transferred from the seller to the buyer. Services are performed for a customer and create value by providing a desired outcome or fulfilling a need.

Meaning of Services

Intangibility: Unlike physical goods, services cannot be seen, tasted, felt, heard, or smelled before they are bought. This makes it difficult for customers to evaluate the service before experiencing it.

Inconsistency (Variability): Services are highly variable and depend on who provides them and when, where, and how. This variability can affect the quality of the service provided.

Inseparability: Services are produced and consumed simultaneously. For example, a haircut or a medical consultation cannot be separated from the service provider. This means the quality of the service is closely linked to the service provider.

Inventory (Perishability): Services cannot be stored for later use. Once rendered, they cannot be returned or reused. For instance, an empty seat on a flight cannot be stored and sold later.

Goods Vs. Services

Goods vs. Services

Goods

Physical, tangible products that can be stored and transported.

Examples: cars, TVs, clothes.

Services

Intangible offerings that are performed for customers.

Examples: banking, haircuts, consulting.

Tangibility: Goods are tangible and can be seen, touched, and stored, whereas services are intangible and cannot be seen, touched, or stored.

Ownership: When purchasing goods, ownership is transferred from the seller to the buyer. In services, there is no transfer of ownership; the buyer pays for the experience or performance.

Involvement: Goods are produced, then sold, and then consumed. Services are sold first, then produced and consumed simultaneously.

Quality Assessment: The quality of goods can be measured and tested before purchase, whereas the quality of services is often subjective and assessed only after consumption.

Characteristics of Services

Characteristics of Services

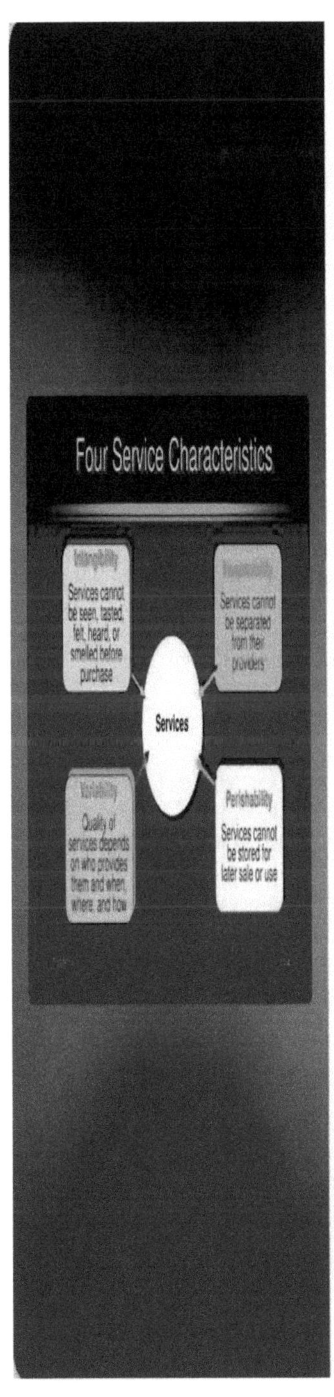

1 — Intangibility

Services cannot be seen, touched, or stored like physical goods.

2 — Inconsistency

The quality of services can vary depending on the provider and circumstances.

3 — Inseparability

Services are produced and consumed simultaneously, often requiring the customer's presence.

1. Intangibility: Services cannot be touched, seen, tasted, or stored. This intangibility makes it challenging to assess service quality before purchase.

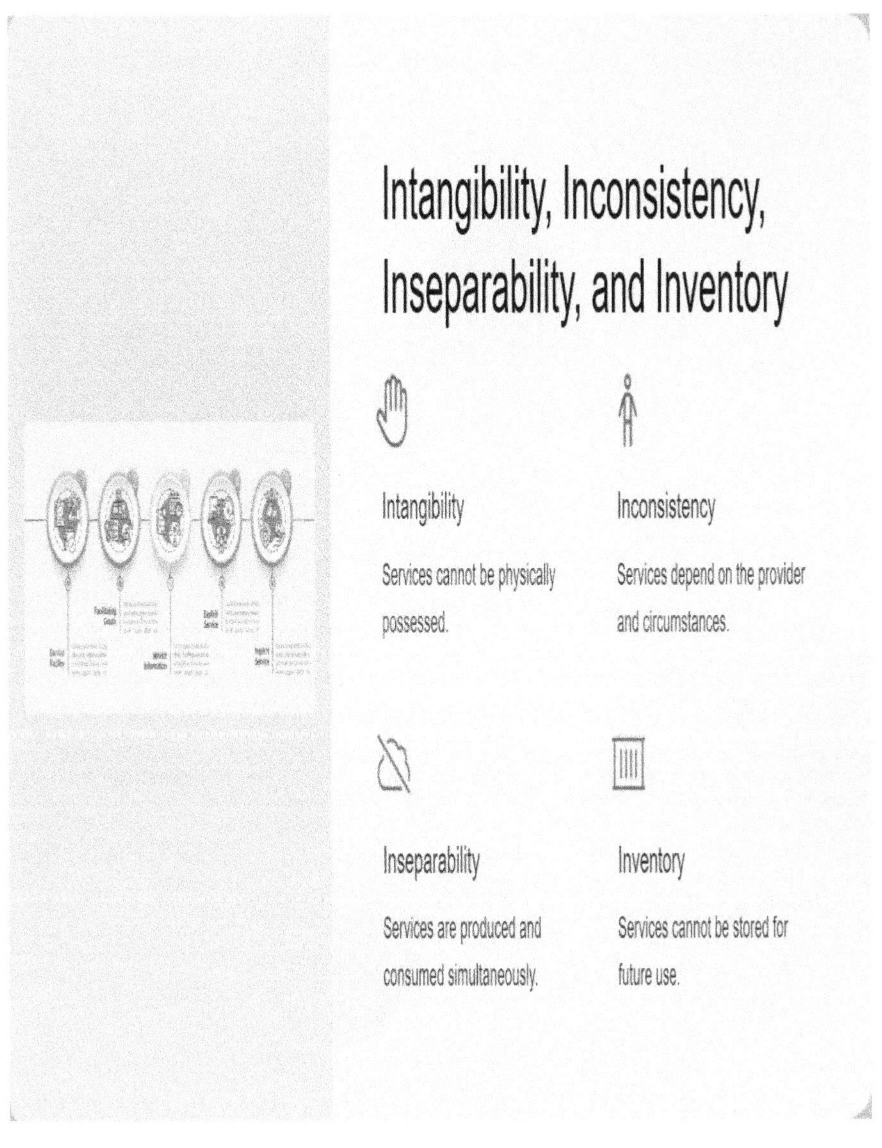

2. Inconsistency (Variability): Services are not uniform and can vary with each delivery due to different factors such as who

provides them, when and where they are provided, and how they are delivered.

3. Inseparability: Production and consumption of services occur simultaneously, meaning the service provider is often present when the service is being consumed, affecting the service outcome.

4. Inventory (Perishability): Services cannot be stored for future use. Once the service is delivered, it cannot be saved for a later date.

Classification of Services

Services can be classified based on several criteria:

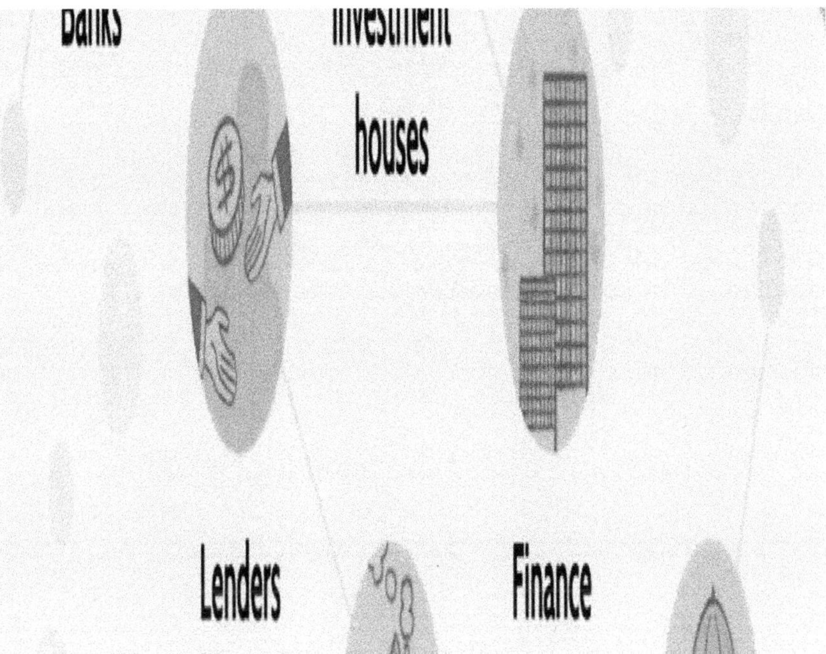

Classification of Services

Producer Services

Services that support business operations, such as accounting, consulting, and IT.

Personal Services

Services that directly benefit individuals, like healthcare, education, and hospitality.

1. By Industry: Healthcare, education, financial services, hospitality, etc.

2. By Nature of Service Act: People-based services (healthcare, education), equipment-based services (transportation, communication).

3. By Type of Client Relationship: Continuous (banking, insurance) vs. discrete (legal services, consulting).

4. By Delivery Method: Services delivered by people (haircut, legal advice) vs. services delivered by machines (ATM, online services).

Growth of the Service Sector in India

The service sector in India has shown remarkable growth and has become a dominant part of the Indian economy. This growth is attributed to several factors:

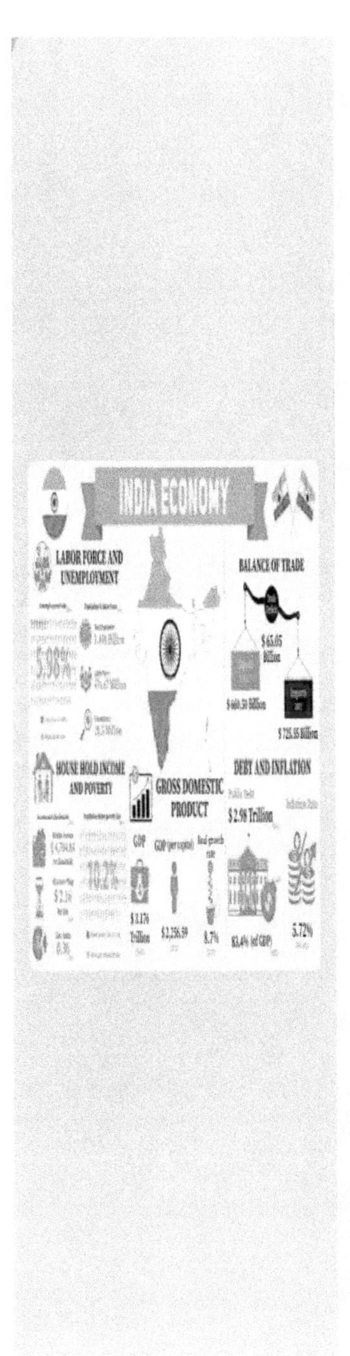

Growth of Service Sector in India

1 Rapid Urbanization

The rise of cities and urban centers has driven demand for services.

2 Technological Advancements

Innovations in IT, telecommunications, and digital services have fueled growth.

3 Rising Middle Class

India's growing middle class has increased consumption of services.

1. Economic Liberalization: Post-1991 economic reforms opened up various sectors to private and foreign investments, enhancing growth opportunities in services.

2. IT and BPO Boom: The rise of Information Technology (IT) and Business Process Outsourcing (BPO) has significantly contributed to the service sector's growth.

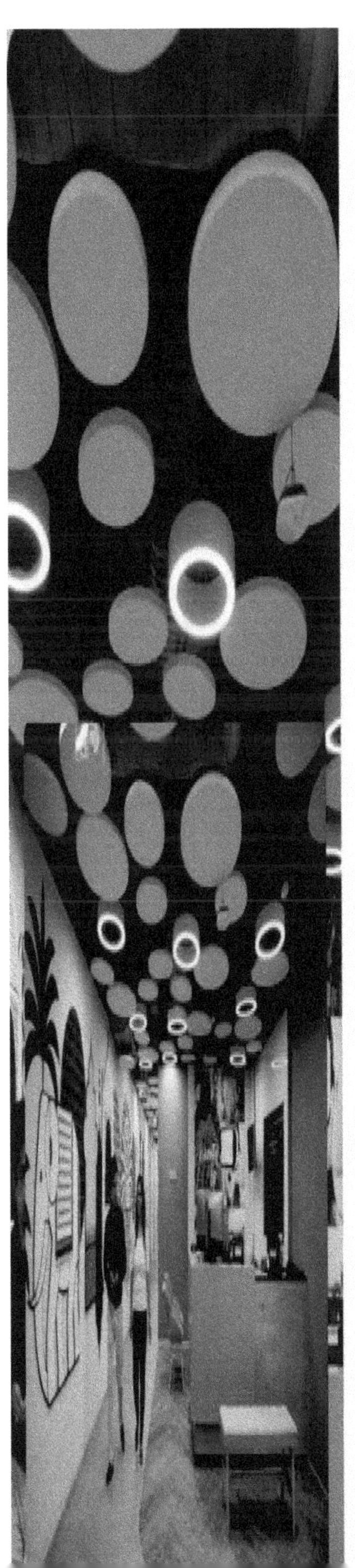

Factors Responsible for Growth of Service Sector in India

Liberalization and Privatization	Opening up the economy and privatizing state-owned enterprises has expanded the service sector.
Foreign Direct Investment	Inflows of FDI have boosted services like IT, finance, and telecommunications.
Rising Education Levels	Educated workforce has enabled

3. Urbanization: Increasing urbanization has led to greater demand for services like healthcare, education, and retail.

4. Rising Income Levels: Higher disposable incomes have increased consumer spending on services such as travel, hospitality, and entertainment.

5. Government Initiatives: Policies aimed at boosting sectors like tourism, healthcare, and education have further spurred growth.

6. Globalization: Increased connectivity and global trade have expanded the market for Indian services, particularly in IT and consulting.

7. Demographic Changes: A growing middle class and a young population have driven demand for new and diverse services.

2

In services marketing if you can build the trust with your people,

they'll do business with you.

Goods Vs Services

Services Marketing Mix: The 7 Ps

The Services Marketing Mix, often referred to as the extended marketing mix, includes seven elements (7 Ps): Product, Price, Place, Promotion, People, Process, and Physical Evidence. These elements help in effectively marketing services.

1. Product

Levels of Service Product

Core Service: The primary benefit or service that satisfies the customer's basic need.

Supplementary Services: Additional services that enhance the core service. These can be facilitating or supporting services.

The Flower of Service

The Core Service

The Essence

The core service is the primary reason a customer is purchasing a service. It represents the fundamental value proposition that meets the customer's core needs. Whether it's providing transportation, financial management, or a dining experience, the core service is the foundational element that forms the basis of the entire service offering.

Defining the Core

Clearly defining the core service is crucial for businesses to establish a strong and focused service proposition. By honing in on the primary customer need and the unique way the organization fulfills it, the core service becomes the bedrock upon which the entire service flower can be built.

Aligning the Petals

The core service acts as the central element around which the facilitating and enhancing services are designed and integrated. Ensuring a seamless alignment between the core and the surrounding petals is essential for crafting a cohesive and compelling service experience.

Developed by Christopher Lovelock, the Flower of Service framework consists of core services surrounded by supplementary services:

Facilitating Services: Information, order-taking, billing, and payment.

Enhancing Services: Consultation, hospitality, safekeeping, and exceptions.

Optimizing the Flower of Services

Understand Customer Needs

1 Conducting thorough market research and deeply understanding the target customer's pain points, preferences, and expectations is the first step in designing an effective flower of services.

Align Services with the Core

2 Carefully aligning the facilitating and enhancing services with the core offering ensures a cohesive and seamless customer experience that meets and exceeds expectations.

Continuously Innovate

3 Regularly reviewing and updating the flower of services, based on evolving customer needs and market trends, allows businesses to stay ahead of the competition and maintain a competitive edge.

Service Blueprint

A service blueprint is a visual representation that maps out the service process, highlighting customer interactions and service delivery.

Components of Service Blueprint

Customer Actions: Steps taken by customers.

Frontstage (Visible Contact) Employee Actions:

 Actions taken by employees in direct contact with customers.

Backstage (Invisible Contact) Employee Actions:

Behind-the-scenes activities.

Support Processes: Internal processes supporting service delivery.

Physical Evidence: Tangible cues that customers encounter during the service process.

Steps in Preparing Service Blueprint

1. Identify the Service Process: Define the service to be blueprint.

2. Map Customer Actions: Outline the steps customers take.

3. Map Employee Actions: Include visible and invisible employee actions.

4. Link Support Processes: Add internal processes that support service delivery.

5. Add Physical Evidence: Include all tangible elements customers come into contact with.

Stages in New Service Product Development

1. Idea Generation: Brainstorming and generating new service concepts.

2. Service Concept Development: Defining the service and its

benefits.

3. Feasibility Analysis: Assessing the feasibility and profitability.

4. Service Design and Testing: Developing service prototypes and testing them.

5. Market Testing: Piloting the service in a limited market.

6. Commercialization: Launching the service to the broader market.

7. Post-Launch Review: Evaluating the service performance and making necessary adjustments.

Service Life Cycle

The Service Life Cycle consists of stages a service goes through from introduction to decline:

1. Introduction: Launch and initial market entry.

2. Growth: Rapid market acceptance and increasing sales.

3. Maturity: Peak sales and market saturation.

4. Decline: Decrease in sales and market presence.

2. Place

Distribution Strategies for Services

Direct Distribution: Direct interaction between service provider and customer (e.g., online services).

Indirect Distribution: Use of intermediaries to deliver the service (e.g., travel agents).

Channels of Distribution in Services

Franchising: Granting the right to use a business model and brand.

Agents and Brokers: Intermediaries that facilitate the service delivery.

Electronic Channels: Online platforms and digital means of service delivery.

Challenges in Distribution of Services

Intangibility: Difficulty in showcasing the service.

Inseparability: Need for simultaneous production and consumption.

Inconsistency : Variability in service delivery.

Perishability: Inability to store services for future use.

3. Promotion

Promotion Objectives for Services

Informing: Educating customers about the service.

Persuading: Convincing customers to choose the service.

Reminding: Keeping the service top-of-mind for customers.

Promotional Tools

Personal Selling: Direct interaction with potential customers.

Advertising: Mass communication through various media.

Sales Promotion: Incentives to encourage service purchase (e.g., discounts).

Services Marketing Triangle

The Services Marketing Triangle highlights the relationships between the company, employees, and customers:

Internal Marketing: Between the company and employees.

External Marketing: Between the company and customers.

Interactive Marketing: Between employees and customers.

4. Pricing

Pricing Objectives

Profit Maximization: Setting prices to achieve maximum profit.

Market Penetration: Setting low prices to attract customers and gain market share.

Market Skimming: Setting high prices to maximize revenue from early adopters.

Pricing Strategies

Market Skimming: High prices initially to maximize revenue from early adopters.

Market Penetration: Low prices to attract a large customer base quickly.

Synchro Pricing: Adjusting prices based on demand and capacity.

Psychological (Odd) Pricing: Setting prices slightly below a round number (e.g., $9.99).

Market Segmentation Pricing: Different prices for different market segments based on willingness to pay.

The 7 Ps framework is crucial for effectively marketing services. Each element plays a significant role in delivering a superior service experience, building customer loyalty, and achieving business objectives. Understanding and strategically applying these elements can lead to successful service marketing and a competitive advantage in the market.

3

Emotions drive customer decisions. Most brand communication focus on customer emotions.

Communication channels

People

Role of Service Employees in a Service Business

Service employees are crucial in delivering a positive customer experience and ensuring service quality. Their roles include:

Frontline Interaction : Direct contact with customers, influencing

perceptions and satisfaction.

Service Delivery: Executing service processes and fulfilling

customer needs.

Customer Support: Assisting and solving customer issues or

queries.

Brand Ambassadors: Representing the company's values and

brand image.

Service Profit Chain

The Service Profit Chain is a model that links employee

satisfaction, customer satisfaction, and profitability. It highlights

the importance of internal service quality in driving business

performance. Key components include:

1. Internal Service Quality: Providing a supportive work environment and resources.

2. Employee Satisfaction: Satisfied employees are more productive and motivated.

3. Employee Productivity: Efficient and effective service delivery.

4. External Service Value: High-quality service perceived by customers.

5. Customer Satisfaction: Satisfied customers are loyal and promote the business.

6. Customer Loyalty: Repeat business and referrals.

7. Profitability and Growth: Increased revenues and market share.

Concept of Service Encounter – Moment of Truth

The service encounter is the interaction between the customer and the service provider. The Moment of Truth is a critical point in the service encounter where customer impressions are formed and service quality is judged. Key aspects include:

First Impressions: Initial contact sets the tone for the entire experience.

Critical Incidents: Specific interactions that significantly impact customer satisfaction.

Recovery Opportunities: Moments where the provider can resolve issues and turn a negative experience into a positive one.

Training and Development of Employees

Effective training and development programs ensure that service employees have the skills and knowledge to deliver excellent service. Key elements include:

Orientation Programs: Introducing new employees to the company's culture, values, and expectations.

Skill Training: Teaching specific job-related skills and procedures.

Customer Service Training: Enhancing communication, problem-solving, and interpersonal skills.

Continuous Development: Ongoing education and training opportunities to keep skills up-to-date.

Physical Evidence

Nature and Importance of Physical Evidence in Services

Physical evidence refers to the tangible elements that customers encounter during a service experience. These elements help customers assess service quality and form perceptions. Key

components include:

Service Environment: The physical setting where the service is

delivered (e.g., décor, cleanliness).

Service Facilities: Tools and equipment used to deliver the service

(e.g., seating, signage).

Service Documentation: Tangible items provided to customers

(e.g., brochures, invoices).

Importance of Physical Evidence

Perception of Quality: Enhances the customer's perception of the

service quality.

Differentiation: Helps differentiate the service from competitors.

Customer Comfort: Creates a comfortable and welcoming environment.

Brand Image: Reinforces the company's brand and values.

Process

Service as a Process & as a System

Services are processes involving a series of activities to deliver value to customers. Understanding service as a system involves:

Service Process: Steps taken to deliver the service (e.g., booking, delivery, follow-up).

Service System: Integrated set of processes and resources working together to provide the service.

Strategies for Managing Inconsistency

Standardization: Establishing standard procedures and guidelines to ensure consistency.

Customization: Adapting the service to meet individual customer needs while maintaining core standards.

Quality Control: Regular monitoring and evaluation of service delivery to maintain high standards.

Customers as Co-Producers of Services

Customers play an active role in the service process, often contributing to the production and delivery of the service. This co-production can involve:

Self-Service: Customers performing tasks themselves (e.g., self-checkout).

Participation: Customers providing input or feedback (e.g., co-designing a product).

Collaboration: Customers working with service providers (e.g., consulting sessions).

Self-Service Technologies (SSTs)

SSTs allow customers to perform services on their own, using technology. Benefits and examples include:

Convenience: Enables customers to access services anytime and anywhere (e.g., online banking).

Efficiency: Reduces wait times and speeds up service delivery (e.g., airport kiosks).

Cost Savings: Lowers operational costs for service providers (e.g., automated customer support).

By effectively managing the elements of the services marketing mix—Product, Price, Place, Promotion, People, Physical Evidence, and Process—businesses can enhance their service delivery, improve customer satisfaction, and achieve their business goals.

4

Service Guarantee

"Service Guarantee is not just about being seen as better than the competition. It's about being trusted as the only solution to customer's problem".

Service Guarantee

Concept of Service Guarantee

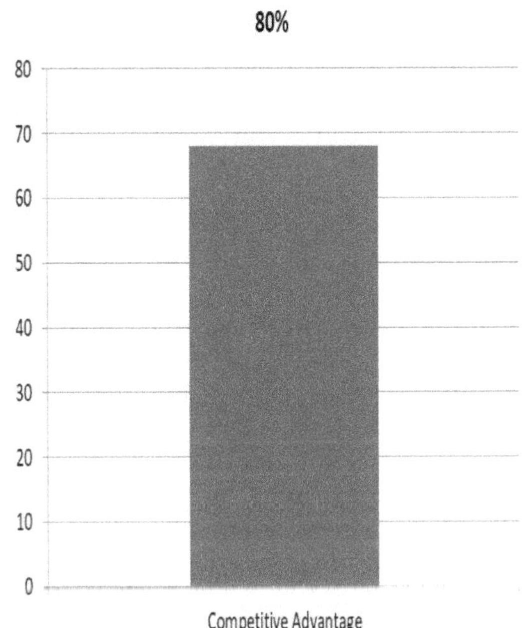

A service guarantee is a formal pledge made by a company to assure customers of the quality and reliability of its services. It typically includes a promise to compensate customers if the service fails to meet predetermined standards. The key aspects of a service guarantee are:

Explicit Promise: Clearly defined terms and conditions outlining the service standards and compensation.

Customer Assurance: Provides customers with confidence in the service quality.

Differentiation: Helps distinguish the service from competitors.

Motivation: Encourages employees to maintain high service standards.

Elements of an Effective Service Guarantee

Unconditional: No strings attached, easy for customers to understand and claim.

Meaningful: Covers important aspects of the service that matter to customers.

Easy to Invoke: Simple and hassle-free process for customers to claim the guarantee.

Credible: Believable and backed by a reliable service delivery

process.

Handling Complaints Effectively

Importance of Handling Complaints

Customer Retention: Addressing complaints effectively can turn

dissatisfied customers into loyal ones.

Service Improvement: Provides valuable feedback for improving

service quality.

Reputation Management: Demonstrates commitment to

customer satisfaction and enhances the company's reputation.

Steps for Effective Complaint Handling

1. Listen Actively: Pay attention to the customer's concerns without interrupting.

2. Empathize: Show understanding and empathy towards the customer's situation.

3. Apologize: Offer a sincere apology for the inconvenience caused.

4. Find a Solution: Work collaboratively with the customer to find a satisfactory resolution.

5. Follow Up: Ensure the customer is satisfied with the resolution and follow up if necessary.

Defects, Failures, and Recovery

Identifying Defects and Failures

Defects: Flaws or shortcomings in the service delivery process that lead to customer dissatisfaction.

Failures: Instances where the service fails to meet customer expectations or promised standards.

Common Causes of Service Defects and Failures

Human Error: Mistakes made by employees during service delivery.

Process Failures: Inefficiencies or breakdowns in the service process.

Technical Issues: Problems with technology or equipment used in service delivery.

External Factors:Uncontrollable events such as weather or supply chain disruptions.

Service Recovery

Service recovery refers to the actions taken by a company to rectify a service failure and restore customer satisfaction. Effective service recovery can enhance customer loyalty and improve overall service quality.

Steps in Service Recovery

1. Acknowledge the Issue: Recognize and admit the service failure.

2. Apologize Sincerely: Offer a heartfelt apology to the customer.

3. Assess the Situation: Understand the root cause of the failure and its impact on the customer.

4. Offer a Solution: Provide a fair and prompt resolution to the problem.

5. Implement Preventive Measures: Make necessary changes to prevent similar failures in the future.

Techniques for Service Recovery

Compensation: Offering refunds, discounts, or complimentary services to make up for the failure.

Empowerment: Allowing employees to make decisions and take actions to resolve issues promptly.

Service Guarantees: Reinforcing the company's commitment to quality and reliability through guarantees.

A well-structured service guarantee, effective complaint handling, and robust service recovery strategies are essential for maintaining high service quality and customer satisfaction. By addressing defects and failures proactively, businesses can enhance their reputation, foster customer loyalty, and drive long-term success.

Differentiation

5-E

Service Quality don't chase customers; they attract customers by providing the authenticity and durability.

Service Quality

Service Quality

Meaning of Service Quality

Service quality refers to the degree to which a service meets or exceeds customer expectations. It is a critical determinant of customer satisfaction, loyalty, and competitive advantage. Service quality can be more challenging to evaluate than product quality due to its intangible nature, variability, and inseparability.

Determinants/Dimensions of Service Quality

Service quality is often assessed through various dimensions that help in understanding and measuring it. The widely accepted dimensions are:

1. Tangibles: Physical facilities, equipment, and appearance of personnel. This includes the cleanliness, layout, and presentation of the service environment.

2. Reliability: The ability to perform the promised service dependably and accurately. This includes consistency and accuracy in service delivery.

3. Responsiveness: The willingness to help customers and provide prompt service. This involves the speed and effectiveness of the service provided to customers.

4. Assurance: The knowledge and courtesy of employees and their ability to convey trust and confidence. This includes the competence and professionalism of the service staff.

5. Empathy: The provision of caring, individualized attention to customers. This involves understanding customer needs and providing personalized service.

54

How Customers Evaluate Service Performance

The Impact of Service Quality

Revenue Growth

Exceptional service quality leads to increased customer loyalty, referrals, and repeat business.

Competitive Advantage

Companies that excel in service quality often differentiate themselves in the market.

Brand Reputation

Positive service experiences foster a strong, customer-centric brand image.

Customers evaluate service performance based on their experiences and perceptions. They compare the actual service received with their expectations. The evaluation process involves:

1. Pre-Purchase Expectations: Customers have certain expectations before experiencing the service, formed by word-of-mouth, personal needs, past experiences, and marketing communications.

2. Service Encounter: During the service encounter, customers assess the performance across various dimensions of service quality.

3. Post-Purchase Evaluation: After the service is delivered, customers compare the perceived service with their initial

expectations. The outcome can be:

- Satisfaction: If perceived service meets or exceeds

expectations.

- Dissatisfaction: If perceived service falls short of

expectations.

Service Quality Models

Gaps Model of Service Quality

The Gaps Model identifies gaps that can cause service quality

problems and influence customer perceptions. The five gaps are:

1. Gap 1 (Knowledge Gap): Difference between customer

expectations and management's perceptions of those

expectations.

2. Gap 2 (Policy Gap): Difference between management's perceptions of customer expectations and the service quality specifications.

3. Gap 3 (Delivery Gap): Difference between service quality specifications and the service actually delivered.

4. Gap 4 (Communication Gap): Difference between service delivery and what is communicated to customers about the service.

5. Gap 5 (Perception Gap): Difference between customer expectations and perceptions of the service delivered. This is the customer gap.

The goal is to identify and close these gaps to enhance service quality and customer satisfaction.

SERVQUAL Model

Dimensions of SERVQUAL

Reliability

Providing consistent, dependable, and accurate service.

Assurance

Inspiring trust and confidence through knowledgeable, courteous staff.

Tangibles

Maintaining modern equipment, facilities, and employee appearance.

The SERVQUAL model, developed by Parasuraman, Zeithaml, and Berry, is a tool for measuring service quality. It focuses on the five dimensions of service quality (tangibles, reliability, responsiveness, assurance, and empathy) and compares customer expectations with perceptions. The SERVQUAL model involves:

1. Survey Development: Creating a questionnaire based on the five dimensions to assess customer expectations and perceptions.

2. Data Collection: Gathering responses from customers regarding their expectations and perceptions of the service.

3. Gap Analysis: Calculating the gap between customer expectations and perceptions for each dimension.

4. Improvement Actions: Identifying areas with significant gaps and implementing strategies to improve service quality.

62

Understanding service quality and its determinants is essential for businesses to meet customer expectations and achieve high levels of customer satisfaction. The Gaps Model and SERVQUAL Model provide frameworks for evaluating and improving service quality. By addressing gaps and focusing on key dimensions, businesses can enhance their service delivery, build customer loyalty, and gain a competitive edge in the market.

6 -F

"Navigating services is the intersection of how one see and how others see"

Managing services

Managing the Demand and Supply of Services

Effective management of demand and supply in services is crucial due to the intangibility, variability, and perishability of services. Proper strategies ensure a balance between demand and capacity, leading to optimized service delivery and customer satisfaction.

Patterns and Determinants of Demand

Patterns of Demand

1. Predictable Demand: Regular, cyclical patterns (e.g., daily, weekly, seasonal).

2. Unpredictable Demand: Irregular and difficult to forecast (e.g., emergencies, special events).

3. Peak Demand: Times when demand exceeds normal levels (e.g., holidays, weekends).

4. Off-Peak Demand: Times when demand is lower than usual (e.g., weekdays, non-holiday periods).

Determinants of Demand

1. Customer Preferences: Vary based on trends, culture, and individual tastes.

2. Price Sensitivity: Higher prices may reduce demand, while discounts and promotions can increase it.

3. Seasonality: Weather and seasons affect demand (e.g., tourism, ice cream sales).

4. Special Events: Festivals, holidays, and events can spike demand.

5. Economic Factors: Income levels, economic conditions, and employment rates influence demand.

6. Competitor Actions: Promotions and pricing strategies of competitors impact demand.

Strategies for Managing Demand

1. Differential Pricing: Using variable pricing to manage demand (e.g., off-peak discounts, peak surcharges).

2. Promotion and Advertising: Encouraging demand during off-peak times through targeted marketing campaigns.

3. Product Modification: Offering variations or additional services to stimulate demand (e.g., special packages, value-added services).

4. Queuing Systems: Managing customer wait times effectively (e.g., appointment scheduling, virtual queues).

5. Reservation Systems: Allowing customers to book services in advance to manage demand flow.

6. Developing Complementary Services: Offering related services that can balance demand (e.g., in-store cafes in retail stores).

Managing the Capacity

Capacity Planning

1. Forecasting Demand: Predicting future demand based on historical data, market trends, and external factors.

2. Resource Allocation: Ensuring adequate staff, equipment, and facilities to meet anticipated demand.

3. Flexibility: Building flexibility into operations to adjust capacity quickly (e.g., part-time staff, temporary facilities).

Waiting Line Strategies

1. Queue Design:Implementing physical and virtual queuing systems to manage customer wait times.

2. Priority Queuing: Offering priority services for certain customers (e.g., VIP customers, loyalty program members).

3. Real-Time Information: Providing real-time updates on wait

times and service status.

4. Comfort and Distraction: Creating a comfortable waiting environment with entertainment, seating, and refreshments.

Inventorying the Demand Through Reservations

1. Reservation Systems: Allowing customers to book services in advance to manage demand and reduce wait times.

2. Overbooking: Accepting more reservations than capacity, anticipating no-shows, to maximize utilization.

3. Deposit and Cancellation Policies: Implementing policies to ensure commitment and manage no-shows (e.g., advance deposits, cancellation fees).

4. Dynamic Adjustments: Adjusting reservation availability based on real-time demand and capacity (e.g., dynamic pricing for reservations).

Managing the demand and supply of services involves understanding demand patterns, implementing effective demand management strategies, and ensuring capacity planning aligns with anticipated demand. By utilizing techniques such as differential pricing, promotion, and reservation systems, businesses can optimize service delivery, enhance customer satisfaction, and achieve operational efficiency.

CASE 1

Brand is a TRUST to customers... a promise of quality, consistency, durability, and reliability.

Kalrock Capital, a London-based asset management company said it, along with UAE investor Murari Lal Jalan has been chosen as the new owners of the bankrupt airline Jet Airways.

"Our consortium was chosen by the committee of creditors in a meeting that concluded this evening," Igor Starha, Managing Director feels.

Another consortium comprising Haryana-based Flight Simulation Technique Centre, Mumbai's Big Charter and Abu Dhabi's Imperial Capital Investments was also in the race. Kalrock's website described it as a London-based asset management company with interests in real estate, venture capital and "special situations". Jalan, through his company MJ Developers, has invested in real estate, mining, trading, construction, FMCG, dairy, travel and tourism.

Jet, India's oldest private carrier, stopped operations in April last year due to a cash crunch and piling debt and was dragged to India's bankruptcy court in June, by its lenders, to whom it owed more than ₹8,000 crore. The process has dragged on since then with several investors throwing their hats in the ring but unable to submit concrete proposals within the deadline. The suitors included South American conglomerate Synergy Group and New Delhi-based Prudent ARC.

Starha said the formal takeover process will begin now and that the conglomerate plans to operate Jet as an Indian carrier. Apart from the flying licence, it will get six Boeing 777 aircraft.

Questio1 What is the case of Jet Airways?

2. What is your opinion of present measures taken for jet airways.Suggest services strategies to be followed.

CASE 2

Services make people's lives better. They simplify decision making, build trust, and establish loyalty.

Shrinking of Food Business -Remodeling Required

The restaurant industry, devastated by layoffs and shutdowns, is looking for a reset. New business models are emerging, with a thrust on cost-cutting, technology and food delivery

Malini Goyal

It was tough. Very, very tough. I wanted to go hide under my bed," feels Ritu Dalmia, chef and owner of Diva Restaurants. She cursed herself for chasing a career that entailed taking responsibility for so many people. Where she had to take such hard decisions. A job, any job, would have been better than this, she thought.

Currently in Milan, Italy, where she runs three restaurants, Dalmia was talking about the toughest moment she faced in the last six months, which saw a pandemic-triggered devastation of India's ₹4.23 lakh crore food services business that employs 7.3 million people. In July, Dalmia handed over termination letters to 100 of her 220 employees. Many had been with her for years. She shut down four of her seven restaurants in India. "My restaurant was my home, but I was left with no choice," she says.

Is there a silver lining? Was there a lesson that was worth learning? "At one level, I am at peace. This consolidation was required. I am grateful for this knock on my face," she says in a thoughtful moment, as we speak on the phone.

Today, commercial viability and cold rationale dictate all decisions. Every rupee counts. From staff to technology, from menu to lease rentals —everything is put under the scanner to push up operational efficiency and cut costs. Dalmia vows that hereon, expansion will be global, not domestic. Her Italian restaurants have been doing fine as the government there offered tax credit and wage subsidy. Even as her booming catering business has shrivelled, new revenue streams are being explored. Dalmia recently launched Diva Casa, a DIY meal kit for home-cooking enthusiasts that comes with instructions and video from Dalmia. "It is doing very well," she says.

Seeing Through the Smoke

Never waste a crisis, they say. It couldn't be truer for restaurateurs in India. Covid-19 has forced people indoors, taking away outdoorsy pursuits like travel and theatres. Cooped up at home, armed with Instagram and Facebook, cooking has emerged as a global pastime and a popular outlet for indulgences. Outside though, the consequences have been disastrous for the restaurant business. Plagued by the pandemic, ignored by the government and panic-struck about an uncertain future, the sector has seen strong waves of layoffs, shutdowns and bankruptcies.

Samir Kuckreja, founder and CEO, Tasanaya Hospitality, says that up to 35% of the organised restaurant business could get wiped out by March 2021. The mortality rate will be sharply higher for the unorganised sector.

Six months after India declared its first lockdown, living with the pandemic is slowly becoming the new normal. Zomato says food delivery recovery is now at pre-Covid levels. Quick service restaurants (QSRs) like McDonald's and KFC have regained 50-60% of their pre-Covid business. "Customers are preferring brands they trust," says Kuckreja.

Foodpreneurs of all shades — from owners of dhabas and roadside kiosks to celebrity chefs and celebrated restaurateurs — have been gasping for survival. They have had to lay off staff, consolidate outlets, prune brands and renegotiate lease rentals. Many are rolling out a range of tweaks to tickle the taste buds of homebound customers. A strong thrust on delivery business runs across formats — from luxury dining outlets at the Taj Hotels to QSRs like McDonald's. There is a big buzz around technology and automation because of the need to offer a contactless experience amid this pandemic. Some, like Gauri Devidayal of The Table in Mumbai, are building on their farm-to-fork differentiation of offering natural and organic produce by launching an app and delivering even in Alibaug ad Pune.

Even in normal times, food business isn't for the fainthearted. The failure rate is unusually high. The past five years have been particularly rough, as the industry reeled from a series of shocks — from demonetisation to GST. The lockdown has been the last nail in the coffin.

However, it may also prove to be an inflection point for the industry. The question is, can it reinvent itself for the digital age where millennials rule? "You become lazy when things are going fine. Crisis makes you more agile," says Anjan Chatterjee, founder of Specialty Restaurants, which has over 100 restaurants across brands like Mainland China and Oh! Calcutta. He has moved to revenue-sharing arrangement with 90% of landlords and is planning 18 new cloud kitchens.

Foodpreneurs, following their passion and chasing flavours, have often struggled to keep a tight focus on their bottom lines. That is changing. Having cried themselves hoarse about the rout, they are looking beyond petitioning the tight-fisted government to craft their future. The smarter ones are retreating into their kitchens to introspect and create new recipes for the future. They are thinking hard about cost economics, staff strength and productivity. "Seismic shifts are underway," says Riyaaz Amlani, CEO, Impresario Entertainment & Hospitality. Most of them acknowledge that whoever survives this storm will emerge stronger and better prepared for the future.

New Course

"We are doing everything we can to keep our heads above the water," says Priyank Sukhija, MD of First Fiddle, which owns brands like Lord of the Drinks and The Flying Saucer. Pre-Covid, it had 25 outlets in seven cities, employing 1,200 people. Today, footfalls stand at 25% of peak capacity. Staff count is 250 with 30-40% salary cut, and the menu has been trimmed from 150 dishes to 50, with zero discounting and ad spends. "We have learnt to be more efficient with fewer staff," says Sukhija. Puff staff and services like attendants in restrooms to hand over tissues and valet parking have been dispensed with. Instead, multitasking is in where managers double as cashiers. Corporate office costs have been slashed by 80% as marketing and accounting have been outsourced.

Delivery business is getting a lot of attention. At McDonald's, while dine-in has yet to pick up, delivery and takeaways are doing very well. "Delivery as a (growth) lever will explode. We are pivoting our entire supply chain to this new behaviour," says Smita Jatia, MD, Hardcastle Restaurants, which is the master franchisee for McDonald's in western and southern India. Even Indian Hotels Company Ltd (IHCL), which runs the luxury chain of Taj Hotels, are betting on delivery to tide over the difficult times. Praveen Chander Kumar, area director of West India, IHCL, and general manager of Taj Lands End, Mumbai, says they have rolled out their own delivery app called Qmin in 10 cities.

For Vineet Manocha, executive group chief, Lite Bite Foods, even as delivery business has grown from 15% to 60% of the total pie, the focus is on exploring new businesses. Lite Bite — which has 23 brands, 218 outlets and 4,500 employees across brands like Punjab Grill and Zambar — foresees the closure of some of its 58-odd outlets at the Mumbai airport.

It is foraying into cloud kitchens, with plans to open 30 in three years. To build a new revenue stream, it has ventured into products like frozen momos and bottled Asian sauces and is also expanding from B-to-B to B-to-C segment. It will soon be rolling out its product offering in Delhi, followed by Mumbai and Bengaluru.

Like everyone else, Amlani too is focused on digitisation, trimmed-down menus, rationalisation of staff costs and multitasking. "Delivery business has seen a growth of 200-300%. Going forward, it will be at the heart of our plan," he says. His chain Smokehouse Deli has seen delivery business trebling from 2-3% in pre-Covid times. Amlani is creating his own delivery ecosystem, including app, fleet of delivery boys and dishes that can travel well. "Aggregator commission is so high that there is no money left on the table," he says.

Meanwhile, AD Singh, MD, Olive Group of Restaurants, is exploring new tie-ups and partners to build a new vertical. "We are re-strategising on a new vision to be a successful delivery business," he says. Even as he tries to sell equity to service his debt, he is "in the process of tying up with a unicorn, looking at food delivery, to open kitchens and delivery channels for our brands. We are looking at 60-70 smaller kitchens in a hub-and-spoke model," he says.

In a sea of hurting entrepreneurs, Maharashtra-based Manu Gulati, founder of craft beer Effingut Breweries, is a breath of fresh air. "I can't stop beaming," he says. The smiles have returned after many painful nights and a business pivot. As pubs closed down, his business ground to a halt. In September, Gulati rolled out a new format — Effingut 2 Go, takeaway growler stations for craft beer. He is adding ready-to-eat food like bar bites and plated meals to the offering. Sticker prices are now one-eighth or even one-tenth of fares in the bar.

The response has been tremendous. As against a monthly target of 1,500 litres, they sold 1,000 litres in five days. The costs have come down, too: if a brew pub costs ₹5 crore and a pub ₹2.5 crore, a growler station costs about ₹30 lakh. The staff count has dramatically reduced. A 200-seater bar would typically have 40-60 employees. Now, just two people can manage a growler station. With the Maharashtra government allowing doorstep delivery of alcohol, they also do home delivery. The new model has improved the company's profit margin — its EBITDA (earnings before interest, taxes, depreciation and amortisation) is up from 15% pre-Covid to 20-25% now. Bullish, Gulati plans to set up 16 growler stations in Maharashtra this fiscal. "The economic toll on our patrons will be huge and they will become tight-fisted. With the takeaway model, we have got something to hold on to," he says.

There is a growing realisation among foodpreneurs that the

restaurant business in India is built on shaky grounds — high rent and low revenue had made it unsustainable even in normal times.

"We need to shatter the pre-Covid business models and disrupt every aspect of our business,"

says Anjan Chatterjee, who started his food business in the 1990s.

"It is like a startup for me," he says about his new steps in the business. The push for more technology and better productivity could see the front-end staff getting reduced by 30% over the long term, he adds.

"The new world is a different world. We are trying to learn," .

Gauri Devidayal

FOUNDER, THE TABLE

BEFORE COVID: Had two restaurants, three delivery brands and an experimental kitchen with 175 employees

COVID IMPACT: Dine-in business ground to a halt as restaurants are still shut

BOUNCE-BACK STRATEGY: Big thrust on food delivery to Alibaug (daily) and Pune (once a week); has launched a delivery app

Manu Gulati,

MD, EFFINGUT BREWERIES

BEFORE COVID: Had six outlets in Maharashtra with 325 employees

COVID IMPACT: With pubs shut and no business, he had to let go of 70% of staff and shutter one outlet

BOUNCE-BACK STRATEGY: Has launched Effingut 2 Go, takeaway growler stations for craft beer, and started home deliveries

AD Singh

MD, OLIVE GROUP OF RESTAURANTS

BEFORE COVID: Had 30 outlets across brands like Olive Bar &

Kitchen, The Fatty Bao and Monkey Bar with 1,450 staff

COVID IMPACT: Little income with high fixed costs, including rising

interest on debt; layoffs of staff

BOUNCE-BACK STRATEGY: Sell equity to service debt, delivery-

friendly menus and tie-up with a unicorn betting on hub-and-

spoke food delivery business

Smita Jatia

MD, HARDCASTLE RESTAURANTS INDIA

BEFORE COVID: Had 320 McDonald's outlets with 10,000

employees in 42 cities

COVID IMPACT: Dine-ins and outlets in malls badly affected

BOUNCE-BACK STRATEGY: Consolidation, with a thrust on drive-

throughs and on-the-go channels where e-orders are delivered to one's car

Ritu Dalmia

OWNER, DIVA RESTAURANTS

BEFORE COVID: Had 7 dine-in restaurants in India and 3 in Italy

with a staff of 220

COVID IMPACT: Closed 4 restaurants in India. Laid off 100

employees

BOUNCE-BACK STRATEGY: Latching on to spurt in home cooking,

she launched Diva Casa that delivers DIY dishes at one's doorstep

"In the long term, we will see focus on business viability,

automation and digitisation"

Samir Kuckreja,

founder & CEO, Tasanaya Hospitality

Riyaaz Amlani

CEO, IMPRESARIO ENTERTAINMENT & HOSPITALITY

BEFORE COVID: 57 restaurants in 16 cities across brands like

Social, Smoke House Deli and Mocha with 3,500 employees

COVID IMPACT: Business has dipped 50-75%

BOUNCE-BACK STRATEGY: Simpler menu, cloud kitchens and a

better delivery ecosystem to cut costs and push sales

Dragonfly Experience, Delhi, has acrylic pods to keep the patrons at a safe distance from each other during Covid-19

"We are learning to be more efficient with fewer staff. We have dispensed with valet parking and restroom attendants"

Priyank Sukhija,

MD, First Fiddle Restaurants

Anjan Chatterjee,

FOUNDER, SPECIALTY RESTAURANTS

BEFORE COVID: Had 109 restaurants, 31 confectioneries and 14 cloud kitchens with over 3,600 staff across brands like Mainland China, Oh! Calcutta & Sigree

COVID IMPACT: Sharp dip in footfall. Moved to revenue-sharing arrangement with 90% of landlords, may close 10% restaurants

BOUNCE-BACK STRATEGY: 18 new cloud kitchens, tech drive to trim staff by 30%, mini kitchens within kitchen

::

"Delivery is here to stay. We are very bullish on the space" "I can't stop beaming. The response to our takeaway model has been terrific. We have got something to hold on to" "We are re-strategising on a new vision to be a successful delivery business. We are in the process of tying up with a unicorn looking at food delivery space" "Pandemic has disrupted personal and professional lives. A new normal is inevitable" "At one level, I am at peace. This consolidation was required. I am grateful for this knock on my face" "Aggregator commission is so high that there is no money left on the table. We are building our own delivery ecosystem" "Crisis makes you more agile. We need to disrupt every part of our business. New world is a different world"

Make a Group of 3 students have online discussions and reply these questions with suggesting new model of food busines.

Q1. What is the story of Malini Goyal, Dalmia and others in the Covid 19 context?

Q2. What are the basic product and supplementary Services in Restaurant Business?

Q3. What remedial measures you suggest to avoid such disruption and recovery of the above services? Suggest new model.

CASE 3

PATRICK and HDI

Patrick is a Vice President of Regional Operations, Pacific Coast, for

Home Designs, Inc. (HDI), one of the world's largest home improvement retailers, operating with over 1,800 stores and other subsidiary companies across North America. The subsidiary companies specialize in flooring, lighting, decorating, plumbing, and landscape supplies. The company focuses on do-it-yourself and professional customers who serve the home improvement, construction, and building maintenance market segments. HDI's strategy is straightforward: To improve margins, invest in the business and increase sales and profits by unleashing the talent of exceptional people.

In addition to their obsession to go the extra mile to make customers happy, HDI also has core values across the organization: teamwork, meritocracy, passion, excellent execution, growth-driven, constructive self-criticism, unquestionable integrity, and social responsibility. Combined with a diverse and inclusive workforce, customer base, and community and vendor relationships, HDI's core values distinguish them from other retailers and gives them a clear competitive advantage.

PROBLEMS IN PATRICK'S REGION

While HDI continues to revolutionize the home improvement industry and strengthen its market position, the same level of success is not being realized in the Pacific Northwest zone, one of Patrick's regions. Patrick just received a quarterly market intelligence report that the Pacific Northwest zone had lost another five percentage points of market share.

Patrick is disappointed, but not surprised. Historically, HDI has dominated the Pacific Northwest region, but over the past three quarters, it has seen steady declines in its customer base and profitability. In addition, stores in the district are increasingly plagued by alternating bouts of stockouts and excess inventory. Patrick and HDI leadership are baffled--these challenges have not been seen in the district before.

The problems permeating the Pacific Northwest zone have frustrated and confused Patrick for months. In fact, finding the root cause has become Patrick's personal mission. He and his staff have painstakingly scrutinized the market research, desperately searching the data for any clue that could identify the source of the problem. However, the more he and his team search, the more they realize the market has not changed-- no new competitors have entered, no current competitors have launched any new initiatives, and construction and home-improvement in the area have not subsided. In fact, the only variable in the whole equation that changed points to a conclusion that Patrick does not want to face.

WHAT CHANGED

Two years ago, Patrick hired a new Zone Manager, Maria Robles, away from a similar position with a major competitor.

He appointed her the lead the Pacific Northwest.

Patrick had once considered Maria to be one of the most impressive candidates he had ever interviewed. Her track record at her former company, albeit brief, was nothing short of spectacular. Having worked as a clerk for the company throughout college and as a Floor Manager during graduate school, she was promoted to Store Manager within a year after earning her M.B.A. Within two years she had risen to a District Manager position (a position quite similar to HDI's Zone Manager job). During her tenure as District Manager, her stores consistently ranked among the company's best in terms of business volume and profitability.

Given these credentials and a seemingly boundless enthusiasm for work, Patrick felt compelled to offer her the job. Although she was still young and relatively inexperienced, his instincts told him that he had found a future superstar and he did not want to lose her to another company. In fact, Patrick has seen her as a protege. He regularly takes her out of her zone and brings her to corporate to get to know the higher-ups in the office.

However, two years later Patrick was beginning to doubt his instincts. Although he did not want to face the ugly truth, he could not escape the fact that all the evidence pointed to ineffective management as the source of the Pacific Northwest's problems. He wondered what had gone wrong. Moreover, the buzz on the grapevine suggested that there was increasing disgruntlement among the members of her team. This just didn't make sense.

Why was such a promising young manager failing to deliver the results that everyone had expected? Was Patrick losing his knack for hiring the right people for the job? How were his boss and HDI's Executive Management Committee going to react to these latest market data?

INVESTIGATING THE SITUATION

Patrick faces his fears and starts to investigate. Maria oversees a team of 15 people, mostly men, who have worked their entire careers at HDI--several recently celebrated their 15th anniversary with the firm. There is a strong bond on the team, developed by shared experience and a deep understanding of the processes and operations of the Pacific Northwest zone.

From employee interviews and observations, Patrick learns that Maria struggles with many of her current staff; she can't quite get traction with them. Patrick gleans particular insight from an interview with Omar Gindele. Like many on the team, Omar has been around for a while. He started with HDI as a contractor, working part-time. He then graduated to a full-time store manager role because of his deep knowledge of the product and customer needs. Patrick really respects Omar's expertise.

Omar relays a conversation he had with Maria last week, to

Patrick. This is the conversation he relayed:

Maria: "Hey guys! Sorry, I'm just popping in, but can you tell me about the customer reaction to the new marketing push? The team at HQ were asking and I said I'd find out for them!"

Omar: "Well I can tell you, but honestly the customers don't seem to care about the marketing all that much when they come in and we can't give them what they're here for!"

Maria: "What do you mean?"

Omar: "For at least the third time this month I have had to turn customers away because we are out of the Deluxe Marble Square Tiling. They come, flyer in hand, and I have to tell them to look online or go over to the next branch because we can't give them what we advertise."

Maria: "Oh dear! Why didn't anyone tell me?"

Omar: "We discussed it at the stand-up meetings Monday and Tuesday, but you were at the 2-day leadership seminar. Sandra, who had the best sales this year, is leaving because she can't stand dealing with our broken promises to these customers."

Maria: "Right, Patrick pulled me for that seminar. And I'm sorry that Sandra is leaving the HDI family! Well, let's get on the phone and order up some more tiles! We want happy customers and flashy floors!"

Omar: "We obviously would have done that if it were that simple. I talked through it with Chris and the other folks in the tiling section. The manufacturer only cuts Deluxe Square Marble Tiles for a week, twice a year. We missed this six-month window when you said we could skip ordering in October because our stock rooms were so full. We can order uncut materials and outsource the cutting if we want to meet our marketing promise but

corporate has never approved that as long as I've worked here.

That's why we ALWAYS order every six months."

Patrick is still unsure how to help Maria. Why would she have

issues getting the support of her team? She's clearly excited and

always comes to the table with lots of new ideas. She has such

great leadership potential.

ANALYZE CASE

Did Patrick really miss the mark with Maria? In a 3-4 paragraph

case analysis essay answer the following questions:

1. What is this case all about?

2. Find out the service gaps in this case.

3. Suggest a solution to this case.

CASE 4

Products are made in the factory, but services are created in the mind.

Imagine shaking hands with a humanoid robot or having artificial intelligence seamlessly integrated into your phone's every function. These a ren't just piped reams any more ; at the Mobile World Congress (MWC) 2024 in Spain, they became tangible realities.

Even jewellery got a tech boost — think smart rings with features that could revolutionise health monitoring and contactless payments.

From the familiar form factors like smartphones reinvented, to completely new categories like robot companions, MWC 2024 painted a picture of a future brimming with exciting possibilities.

Here are some of the top highlights:

1. A WRAPAROUND PHONE

Still at the concept stage, the bendable phone showcased at the Motorola booth is straight out of a sci-fi movie. This is a smartphone that can be moulded into different shapes and can even wrap around your wrist, opening up an entirely new avenue for wearable tech.

The concept sets a new benchmark in smartphone design, taking it far beyond the current foldable designs in the mainstream. The bendable concept can b e propp ed up at va rious angles, like a tent or a stand, and the user interface adjusts dynamically to accommodate the form factors.

Smartwatches have already become ubiquitous and almost a wardrobe staple. Shape-shifting smartphones wrapped around the wrist can be the next intriguing fashion statement. However, questions around comfort during extended wear still remain, which is perhaps why this is still only at the concept stage.

2. AI-POWERED HUMANOID

MWC gave us a first-hand look at an incredible life-like humanoid that can answer questions, hold a conversation, even have some jokes to tell. While such robots are not quite new, Ameca standing at the Etisalat booth has been brought to life using artificial intelligence.

The humanoid has almost life-like facial expressions, especially the eyes that are capable of conveying emotions. Ameca was also quite witty with its replies, its conversational skills powered by OpenAI's GPT-4, the most advanced conversational AI model right now. It had an answer for almost anything, even complimented a visitor's dress, recognising the colour and style.

Created by UK-based Engineered Arts, Ameca is being claimed as the world's most advanced humanshaped robot. Just don't ask what it eats, but in case you are wondering, it's microchips.

3. USING AI IN REAL TIME

Imagine conjuring up any scene or product, real or merely just possible, with just a few touches on your smartphone, and then witnessing it in front of you. That's exactly what I did with a demo phone at the MediaTek booth, with instantaneous results.

Using an AI engine that can dynamically create images in real-time based on text prompts, I conjured up Tim Cook promoting Android phones, just by spelling it out in as many words. AI processors in the present-present-generation mobile chipsets are capable of dishing out such results in realtime, allowing users to instantly visualise their ideas and concepts.

But Generative AI can do even more. A second device had AI summarising a long report into digestible bullet points, which on the surface, looked accurate, while another generated videos from text prompts. 4. SEE-THROUGH LAPTOP

Perhaps the coolest piece of technology I saw at MWC 2024 was the transparent laptop on display at the Lenovo booth. While its utility still eluded me, it nonetheless seemed straight out of a Black Mirror episode. You can peer through the transparent screen of this concept notebook and let the screen not be a distraction from observing the world outside. The laptop uses a microLED display that goes semitransparent when the pixels are turned off, but becomes more and more opaque when the display

lights up.

This translucent display aside, the laptop also had a completely

flat touch keyboard instead of physical keys, adding to the sci-fi

touch. While its use case may not quite be mass-market, it can

perhaps appeal to digital artists who can see the world through

the screen while sketching it.

5. AN AI ASSISTANT

Move over smartphones. It's time for wearable, AI-powered

assistants that can see all and tell all. At the Qualcomm booth at

MWC, an AI Pin from the Silicon Valley-based startup Humane

was unveiled. The device clips to your shirt, has a camera to scan

the world around, and uses generative AI to answer questions.

There's no screen, but a tiny laser projects text onto your palm

that one can interact with. The Humane AI Pin is the answer to smartphone addiction, stripping the computer to its bare essential needs, while keeping its utility and mobility intact.

The technology is designed to fetch your emails and appointments and quench your curiosity about the world around you. For one, it could tell that I was standing at the Qualcomm booth by scanning the signage and described the surrounding as being an indoor exhibition. That said, the gadget did feel like a work in progress. For one, each response was peppered with long pauses, which is understandable because most of the AI is handled on the cloud, but it was slowed even further by the event's spotty connectivity.

Q. What is the influence of AI in Retail Services?.

CASE 5

Swiss pharma major Novartis made a brief announcement that

it had started a "strategic review" of its listed entity, Novartis India Limited, which includes an assessment of its shareholding in the subsidiary.

Exactly three months ago, UK biggie AstraZeneca had also announced it was exiting manufacturing in India as part of a "global strategic review''.

These announcements follow a pattern in which pharma biggies like Pfizer, Sanofi, AstraZeneca and GSK have reduced manpower and trimmed operations in core functions like manufacturing, sales and marketing over the past few years. Some of them have a rich heritage in India, dating back up to 100 years. So, why are they reducing their exposure in the Indian market, where they vied for a toe-hold not so long ago?

Costs, Competition, Patents

India is a Rs 2 lakh-crore-plus market with some of the most pressing health challenges, but increasing competition, higher operational costs and a less viable business have forced MNCs to rethink their strategies. They have been focusing on core competencies and divesting non-core assets, especially after Covid.

So, from an earlier strategy of manufacturing in India they have transitioned to licensing and marketing agreements. Over the years, Novartis, Roche, Eli Lilly and Pfizer tied up with domestic firms like Torrent, Lupin, Cipla and Glenmark for major therapies. Novartis, for instance, recently divested its highgrowth ophthalmology brands to Mumbai-based JB Chemicals for a little over Rs 1,000 crore.

Some MNCs are concerned about India's intellectual property regime, which discourages evergreening of patents and can impose compulsory licensing – allowing a third party to manufacture a drug without the patent owner's consent. So, without fully exiting the country, they have been reducing exposure by truncating portfolios, and avoiding fresh investments. "Faced with regulatory headwinds, IPR challenges and pressure from the parent on generating profits/ value from their Indian businesses, most MNCs are reevaluating their strategy for the Indian market," says Ranjit Shahani, former vicechairman of Novartis India.

Moving Up The Value Chain

Innovation-driven companies are thinning conventional portfolios of generics in a bid to focus on high-value therapeutics like cancer treatments. "Pharmaceutical industry is inherently global, and companies may be redistributing resources to markets with higher growth potential or more favourable business environments," says Utkarsh Palnitkar, independent consultant, life sciences. "Shifting priorities might prompt MNCs to reduce their exposure in certain markets, including India,'.

Under a global reassessment, some MNCs are shedding their

branded generics. This may involve distribution partnerships, sale of manufacturing facilities or legacy high-value brands to domestic biggies, and pruning R&D to enhance efficiency. For instance, Novartis partnered in 2022 with Hyderabad-based Dr Reddy's Labs (DRL) for sale and distribution of its heritage brands like pain medication Voveran. It also divested cardiac brands – Cidmus to DRL for roughly Rs 463 crore and Azmarda to JB Chemicals for Rs 246 crore. In 2017, Torrent had bought its gynaecology medicines.

Pharma MNCs in India have diverse growth strategies and business models. Anil Matai, director general of OPPI (Organisation of Pharmaceutical Producers of India), which represents pharma MNCs, says some have comprehensive portfolios of general medicines across therapy areas, and mega brands with a strong equity, others focus on a differentiated portfolio, while some MNCs focus on large innovator brands, deriving quick growth from co-marketing partnerships with

Indian players.

Shifting Regulatory Sands

Pricing regulations and a complex approval process are among the regulatory challenges pharma firms have faced in India. GlaxoSmithkline India's profits plunged by over 70% in the third quarter results of FY 2023-24, in the wake of price caps on two marquee antibiotic brands, T-Bact and Ceftum, presumably due to their inclusion in the latest revision of National List of Essential Medicines. Sanofi might also be hit with its anti-diabetic Lantus included in the List.

Frequent alterations in regulations can impact the profitability and predictability of operations, leading companies to reconsider their involvement in the market, industry experts say.

Over 9,000 Players In Game

Although India's organised pharma retail market is valued over Rs 2 lakh crore, more than 9,000 companies are jostling in it. So,

MNCs may find it challenging to compete on pricing and market penetration, especially for generic drugs.

"Indian pharmaceutical market has become increasingly competitive, with both domestic and international players vying for market share. Companies such as DRL, which hitherto had a sharper focus on exports, seem to have rediscovered the Indian market. But in overall value terms, the Indian domestic market is not that attractive yet," Palnitkar adds.

That's why some MNCs prefer to leverage local expertise and established networks of domestic companies for marketing and distribution, instead of maintaining a direct presence. This way they don't need to make substantial investment in infrastructure.

This model has been becoming popular. Recently Glenmark tied up with Pfizer for a chronic skin medication, while Dr Reddy's acquired the rights to distribute a 'first-in-class' breast cancer drug from the US biggie. Similar deals have been brokered for lifestyle ailments like diabetes between MNCs and domestic firms.

Develop-In-India Model

In an evolving pharma landscape backed by digitisation and IT, MNCs like Novartis, Roche and AstraZeneca have set up global capability centres in India. These focus on data analysis, designing clinical trial protocols and employing immersive technologies. For instance, a major part of the development of Entresto (sacubitril/valsartan), Novartis' blockbuster cardiac drug, was done at its Hyderabad centre.

It's not that high-end innovator companies have lost interest in India, but they are trying new business models, says Sujay Shetty, partner and pharma leader, PwC India. "Perhaps, over the years, we could see newer marketing models evolve in the Indian market, involving super-specialised importers or even contract marketers," he says.

Impact On Patient

With domestic biggies being agile with rolling out affordable versions of innovator medicines, the patient may not have to worry much. Besides, for speedier access to pricier next-gen treatments, the government could formulate an innovative model which could serve the interests of all stakeholders, including the patient and MNCs.

Q. How services to customers can be consistent during such movements of MNCs from one country to other country?

CASE 6

One of the legacies of the 2020 pandemic and the resulting

lockdowns is the long list of retailers who've filed for bankruptcy.

In the United States, the list of causalities includes Lord & Taylor,

Neiman Marcus, Pier One, Brooks Brothers, Sur La Table, Guitar

Center, and Stein Mart. During this same period, as consumers

have increased their reliance on online shopping, Amazon's share

price has risen from $1,900 to $3,160. Will the end of the

pandemic bring a surge of business to retailers? Will online

grocery shopping become the norm? Can anything slow Amazon's

path to world domination?

To make sense of the long-term impact of the changes we've seen

in 2020, HBR spoke with Marc-Andre Kamel, a Paris-based partner

who heads the global retail practice at Bain & Co. Here are edited

excerpts from that interview:

One view that's been repeated frequently during 2020 is that the pandemic tended to accelerate existing trends, rather than start entirely new ones. Is that true in retailing?

Absolutely. The world of retail was already going through extreme turbulence, driven by a number of factors. The first is consumer behaviors and demographic changes — more single parent households, more people living alone, more urban living. This is a 20-year trend.

On top of that, you have changing expectations — for more quality, more convenience, more speed, more choice, more value, all at the same time. That creates an impossible economic equation for retailers.

At the same time, the market has been rocked by the emergence of disruptive business models. You have, on one hand, the "monster ecosystems," like Amazon and Alibaba, but there are also smaller disruptors in every category. In apparel, for instance, you now have more ability to rent clothing, and there's been growth in second-hand apparel. That's just one example.

Beyond the ecosystems like Amazon and Alibaba, what other types of retailers are well-positioned?

We see four other archetypes that have sustainable positions. One is what we call "regional gems": They are companies that are doing well in local markets. They are protected by having very strong ties to the consumer base and a good value proposition. For instance, there are strong retailers in countries like Portugal, Switzerland, and Russia, where Amazon does not have a strong presence. Eventually these companies may be challenged by a new business model emerging — we can't be sure they will survive — but right now their strategy is working.

The second is what we call "hitchhikers," who ride on the back of platforms. They are typically highly creative, branded retailers with great consumer appeal (think Burberry or Lacoste, for instance) or successful food retailers (think Monoprix or Morrison's) that are not big enough to sustain the fight on technology on their own, so they choose to sell through the ecosystems and piggyback on that growth.

The third model that's doing well is the "value players" —

companies for whom reducing cost and keeping prices low are in

their DNA. Aldi, Trader Joe's, Primark, and TJ Maxx are examples

of that.

The final archetype is the "scale fighters." They are companies

that have enough size to try to fight the ecosystems. Walmart is

one example, although it's trying to become an ecosystem itself.

So those archetypes are how we see the retail world, and some of

them have done relatively well through the pandemic.

What about the companies that aren't well positioned?

We call those the "legacy laggards." Their challenge is to run the company and change the company at the same time. That's very difficult, and Covid has only increased that challenge. We believe that in the United States and Western Europe, more than one in three retailers falls into this category. These companies struggle to maintain profitability. They face market pressure and shareholder pressure. They strip out cost to try to preserve margins, reducing investment, which can exacerbate their problems. Generally, these companies go through consolidation or they fail. These include many companies have filed for bankruptcy in 2020, including household names like Lord & Taylor, JC Penney, and Neiman Marcus in the U.S., and Debenhams, Arcadia, and many others in Europe.

The legacy laggards are the most visible retailers that are struggling, but there's another category that we call "unsustainable innovators." These are companies that launch something exciting in the digital space but have no real path to profitability. As they grow, either they fail or they get acquired. As they grow, either they fail or they get acquired by scale fighters

who learn from them. Jet.com, which was acquired by Walmart, is

an example of that.

Some people hope for a strong retail rebound as societies become

vaccinated, based on the idea that there's pent-up demand to go

shopping. Is that a reasonable hypothesis?

There are two conflicting signals. One is demographic. Gen Z has a

different approach to consumerism than older generations. They

are also less focused on conspicuous consumption, and more on

sustainability and meaning. Covid accelerated this trend and

made it more cross-generational. These forces would lead one to

believe that in the long run, we'll see less of a rush for

consumption.

The conflicting signal comes from China, which came out of the lockdown faster than the Western world. China did experience a retail surge after lockdown. It lasted around three or four months and was more online than offline. Traffic in malls is still a little depressed, but conversion is higher — people who go to stores are more likely to buy. By the end of 2020, retail growth will be positive in China — the additional buying it's seen since lockdown has more than made up for business lost during lockdown. Luxury brands are selling especially well post-

lockdown — some are up 40 to 50% — but Chinese consumers were already the leading buyers of luxury goods before the pandemic, so it's difficult to draw conclusions from the repatriation of some of their global purchases.

The lockdowns and panic-buying led some people to rethink grocery shopping habits. What long-term effect will that have on grocery retailing?

Even before the pandemic, when it came to eating, people were making tradeoffs between time and money. You had a lot of people eating ready-to-eat, and fewer people cooking. That's more expensive on a unit basis, but they're saving time. And out-of-home food consumption was growing quickly. In some Western countries, people were already spending more than 50% of their food budget on restaurants and takeout, rather than on groceries.

How much will the pandemic change those trends? Some argue that this experience allowed people to rediscover cooking and enjoying meals at home with the family. There may be a segment of people who discovered cooking as a hobby during the pandemic, but our research suggests 90% of people want to be able to go to restaurants again. When lockdown ended here in Europe, people rushed to restaurants. So I'm not sure the split between grocery spending and restaurant spending is going to be dramatically affected long-term.

I do expect more people to continue buying groceries online, because it's convenient.

As a consultant, how do you help the legacy laggards who are your clients?

It is possible for a company to still shake itself from this trajectory. It all starts with differentiation and a value proposition that is tailored to the target customer segment you want to delight.

Take one example: department stores. I don't think department stores will completely disappear. There is value in creating an edited assortment for customer segments looking for the editing and curation that department stores bring. Many of these big retailers that are failing have lost sight of who the customers are they want to delight. They try to delight everyone, but they fragment their resources and wind up delighting no one.

So one of the things we do with laggard retailers is help clarify their ambition and identify the customer target they are going after. Once they understand that, they can think more broadly about reinventing their value proposition. In some cases, this might involve selling not just products, but services. In some cases, it might involve partnering with another company to become stronger. I do think we're in the beginning of a big consolidation cycle in retail. Some companies will fail and disappear, but retail is sticky. Instead of failing, we'll see companies getting together.

Can anything stop the growth of the ecosystems?

There's one number I use to put this in perspective: Between 2019 and 2024, Amazon will invest $100 billion more in IT than any of the other top 10 retailers in the world. When you're competing against a company that can spend like that, and which has a history of successful

innovation, it's not a fair fight. This is part of what will drive consolidation.

Amazon has two audiences — the consumers who buy from it, and the smaller businesses that sell through it. People recognize Amazon's success with consumers; during 2020 it's also doubled the number of businesses that transact on its platform.

At the same time, not everything is rosy. In the United States, Amazon had periods where it could not deliver items on time. Its customer experience went down during some periods in the pandemic. So there are limitations on fast growth.

Question Discuss the shift of digital landscape of services marketing.

CASE 7

Vipasha Malhotra's digital clout is a case study. The singer-songwriter gained fame through her Instagram Reels during the pandemic, amassing a following of 175,000 on the Meta-owned platform till now. What's unusual is that the 20-something musician has fetched three times as many subscribers on YouTube in much less time. Typically, content creators, who start on Instagram, struggle to attain a similar following when they move to YouTube. "All I did was cross-post my 15-second clips for Instagram as YouTube Shorts," says the creator from Delhi. "While the launch of Reels resulted in a sudden spike in followers for many creators initially, the growth in subscribers from Shorts has been unbelievably high,

In the race to be the preferred space in creator economy, YouTube has always had a head start. As of September 2023, YouTube has

518 million monthly active users (MAUs) in India compared with Instagram's 244 million, according to Comscore data sourced by ET.

In 2010, when Kevin Systrom and Mike Krieger launched Instagram as a photosharing app, YouTube had already been sharing ad revenue with content creators for three years. By the time Instagram announced Snapchat-like Stories feature on its app, YouTube was on its way to introducing yet another means for creators to monetise their content. In 2017, YouTube launched Super Chat, a way for fans to pay a YouTuber during a live stream. In 2018, Insta tried to take on YouTube by launching IGTV for long-form videos, only to shut it down four years later.

For almost a decade, YouTube dominated the global creator economy, while Instagram was where people shared personal aspects of their lives through static images. The surge of TikTok-inspired short videos transformed this landscape, prompting Instagram's shift from a social network to a content platform catering to our ever-dwindling attention spans. The growing popularity of Instagram influencers gave rise to a conflict between short-form creators and long-form OGs.

Now, with Shorts gaining momentum and homegrown TikTok imitations falling by the wayside, YouTube and Instagram have emerged as the main rivals in India's creator space, competing for greater control of our scrolling habits. Instagram now allows paid subscriptions for creators and has extended its Reel time limit to 90 seconds.

YouTube has recently opened up ad-revenue-sharing for Shorts and launched other fan-funding features like Super Thanks and channel membership. As both platforms introduce feature after feature to outdo each other's impact, creators assess which of the two is better for a sustainable career in content.

Surprisingly, Malhotra maintains her focus on Instagram, despite having a significantly larger subscriber base on YouTube. She says the surge in subscribers did not translate into similarly high viewership for her longer videos. "If I received 500,000 views on Shorts, the view count for longer videos would hover around 10,000. On Instagram, my Reels typically garner over 100,000 views on average, which gets me better brand deals."

the audience for Shorts differs from that for long-form videos. On Instagram, she says, the majority of users are there to consume "short-form content".

WHERE INSTA ACES

Advertisers aiming urban Gen Z and millennials are increasingly spending on Instagram's ad options, says Nikita Abhanave, digital media specialist and podcast host. "Most ads are designed with the short-video format in mind. Longform ads are created only occasionally, usually by brands aiming to establish an emotional connection with the audience," she adds.

Most creators ET spoke to felt that YouTube Shorts lacked original content. Even though a lot of Reel trends are essentially TikTok hand-medowns, original India trends do originate on Reels.

Meanwhile, we have yet to see major internet trends that can be traced back to YouTube Shorts.

In an email correspondence with ET, Ishan John Chatterjee, director, India at YouTube, says, "YouTube is a unique space and we are in our own lane. We are not a social network or a traditional broadcaster. We are really focused on the video experience across screens and formats, and being the best home for video creators, and viewers—period." Instagram declined to participate in the story.

Instagram's coveted blue tick, now available for a fee, is often the epicentre of conversations in the creator economy. Peers also track comments by verified celebrities—which show up prominently—under their rivals' posts. In the digital landscape, these metrics shape the narrative around online influence.

In the first episode of the June 2023 Netflix series, Social Currency, a large screen at the show's entrance displays the participating creators' rankings based on their Instagram follower count, even though some had more YouTube fans. Fazila Allana, producer of the show and joint MD of Sol Productions, says, "We chose their Instagram following because it is more widely discussed. When pitching creators to brands for a campaign, their Instagram figures are checked first—perhaps because brand managers are also on Instagram as it's a social media platform." Be it in reality shows or streaming films such as Kho Gaye Hum Kahan, contemporary culture now pictures content creator as a lifestyle and entertainment influencer on Instagram.

Anushka Rathod, who creates content primarily around finance, says that 95% of her creator identity is tied to Instagram. "For an infotainment creator like me, it's harder to build a personal connection with my audience on YouTube because one cannot show one's personal life the way one can through pictures and stories on Instagram," she says. Rathod has 577,000 YouTube subscribers and 843,000 Instagram followers.

Vimoh, a content creator who primarily debunks misinformation these days, prefers Instagram Reels over 60-second YouTube Shorts for a peculiar reason. "Since Reels can be 90 seconds now, it is convenient to play a 60-second clip filled with misinformation and then use the remaining 30 seconds to challenge it with facts. For YouTube Shorts, you have to edit it further," he says. Vimoh, who prefers to go by his digital avatar instead of his real name, has 178,000 followers on Instagram and a mere 15,000 subscribers on YouTube. Yet, the bulk of the money comes from the latter, he says, in the form of ad revenue, Super Chats and channel membership.

Vimoh's experience, "YouTube has a considerably advanced comment moderation system. This platform allows YouTubers to permanently hide comments from specific users, in addition to having an automated process that identifies and relegates abusive comments to the spam category." While Instagram has also implemented various mechanisms for comment moderation, Vimoh says there is an imperative need to enhance its content moderation system. "Also, when I report something for hate speech, there's rarely any action taken," he says. Most other creators note that both platforms have a lot of ground to cover when it comes to checking misinformation and hate speech.

WHERE YOUTUBE LEADS

Abhanave, the digital media specialist, says YouTube's 'Skip Ad' feature enables brands to consider user behaviour and avoid interfering with their viewing experience. She says ads should flow smoothly to prevent users, particularly urban Gen Z, from reporting them, which they are known to do on other platforms that lack a 'skip ad' option, for a cleaner feed experience.

Pulkit Kochar, a creator whose Reels on Bollywood trivia have garnered him 55,000 Insta followers, has been trying to shift to YouTube ever since his Insta following stagnated. "Most of my viral Reels get 10% views from followers while 90% are non-followers who watch, like and move on. Instagram gives you fame faster than YouTube, but on YouTube there's a higher chance of getting discovered through search even if the algorithm doesn't push your video," he says. Kochar made a few cameos on YouTube in 2014 when he was a tad camera-shy. "People still remember me for those cameos. After becoming more active on Instagram, I often encounter people who recognise me but can't recall where they have seen me," adds Kochar.

Aanam C recently ran into someone who kept telling the beauty creator that she had "seen her on Instagram so many times". "I could tell that she couldn't remember my name. That's short-form content for you," says Aanam, who has 337,000 Instagram followers and about the same number of YouTube subscribers. "We live very strange lives where it seems like we are talking to millions but we are effectively talking to a phone. Human interactions are quite precious to us so encounters like these leave a huge impact,"

Aanam appreciates the stability of YouTube's organic earnings, enabling her to decline certain Instagram brand deals on principle—even if the said deal surpasses a month's YouTube earnings. "I like that Shorts now allows us to embed a link to a longer video at the bottom of a clip, marked by its distinctive 'play' icon. This feature can guide short-form audiences toward long-form content," she says.

That said, today's creators, having witnessed the class wars between TikTokers and YouTubers, no longer engage in platform battles, says Anshu Patni, a content coach. "Many creators have matured and realised the unpredictability of platform dynamics. Instagram creators face challenges of income beyond brand deals, while YouTubers, often with a less upscale audience than Instagram influencers, grapple with establishing their 'face value'. However, those who invested in longform storytelling are sustaining careers as writers, producers and showrunners now,"

Ultimately, both platforms roughly have a 50% overlap, creators reckon. "If not for Instagram, a lot of us would not have found a new audience for our content," says Ankita Shrivastav, a standup comedian who began her digital journey with longform videos on YouTube in 2017 and became active on Insta only during the pandemic. She has half a million followers/ subscribers on either platform now. "I've noticed that crafting Reels from my YouTube standup content resonates most effectively with my Instagram audience. The resulting popularity on Instagram not only draws in brands but also provides the financial backing for me to invest in producing extensive comedy content," says Shrivastav. "In every field, you have to align and adapt. Here, that involves learning how to use short-form videos to sustain your career in long-form content,"

Question : Discuss influence of social media on services marketing.

Bibliography

1. Hatch, M. J. (2017). The dynamics of organizational identity. Routledge.

2. Schultz, M., Hatch, M. J., & Larsen, M. H. (2000). The expressive organization: Linking identity, reputation, and the corporate brand. Oxford University Press.

3. Aaker, D. A. (1991). Managing brand equity: Capitalizing on the value of a brand name. Free Press.

4. de Chernatony, L. (2010). From brand vision to brand evaluation: The strategic process of growing and strengthening

brands. Routledge.

5. Fombrun, C. J., & Van Riel, C. B. (2004). Fame & fortune: How successful companies build winning reputations. Financial Times Prentice Hall.

6. Keller, K. L., & Lehmann, D. R. (2006). Brands and branding: Research findings and future priorities. Marketing Science, 25(6), 740-759.

7. Olins, W. (2003). On brand. Thames & Hudson.

8. Ind, N., & Coote, L. (2004). Branding and advertising. SAGE Publications.

9. Kapferer, J. N. (2004). The new strategic brand management: Creating and sustaining brand equity long term. Kogan Page Publishers.

10. Aaker, D. A., & Joachimsthaler, E. (2000). Brand leadership. Simon and Schuster.

11. Aaker, D. A. (1996). Building strong brands. Simon and Schuster.

12. Hatch, M. J., & Schultz, M. (2010). Toward a theory of brand co-creation with implications for brand governance. Journal of Brand Management, 17(8), 590-604.

13. Keller, K. L. (1993). Conceptualizing, measuring, and managing customer-based brand equity. Journal of Marketing, 57(1), 1-22.

14. Kotler, P., & Keller, K. L. (2016). Marketing management. Pearson.

15. Kapferer, J. N. (2012). The new strategic brand management: Advanced insights and strategic thinking. Kogan Page Publishers.

16. Balmer, J. M. T., & Greyser, S. A. (2003). Revealing the corporation: Perspectives on identity, image, reputation, corporate branding, and corporate-level marketing. Routledge.

17. Davis, D., & Dunn, M. (2002). Building a successful brand: Branding basics. Journal of Business Strategy, 23(4), 26-31.

18. Fombrun, C. J. (1996). Reputation: Realizing value from the corporate image. Harvard Business Press.

.

Times of India

Economic Times

The Hindu

The New York Times

The Financial Times

HBR (Harvard Business Review)

ABOUT THE AUTHOR

Dr. Shyam Shukla has been a faculty at Linnaeus University, Sweden. He is presently Senior Faculty at Bharati Vidyaoeeth (Deemed to be University) Institute of Management and Entrepreneurship Development Pune. He had been Dean-Industry Institute Interaction and former Director & Principal in-charge of the Central Institute of Business Management Research & Development Nagpur. Dr. Shyam Shukla is also Executive Chairman of International Centre for Spiritualism and Leadership. Dr. Shyam Shukla had been founder member and President of National Human Resources Development Network, Nagpur Chapter. Dr. Shyam Shukla is also a member of Decision Sciences Institute USA. He is also Chairman Nagpur Region for Association of Management of MBA/MMS Institute (AMMI) Pune. Dr. Shyam

Shukla did his Masters & Ph. D. in Business Administration. Dr. Shyam Shukla further specialized himself in the area of International Business, Environmental Engineering and Public Relations. Dr. Shyam Shukla authored four books on International Business and Research Methodology . Dr. Shyam Shukla worked for many organizations like Golf Course Delhi, Birla Global Asset Fin Co. Ltd, Professional C&F, Ashok Leyland etc pan India., Dr. Shyam Shukla has also been instrumental in providing consultancy services and training programs with many organizations. Dr. Shyam Shukla has conducted many training workshops and seminar on HRD & Women Empowerment. Dr. Shyam Shukla believed in empowering the youths with the knowledge of getting global and imparting them with the knowledge of Foreign Trade. Dr. Shyam Shukla is also acquainted with Psychometric Testing, Neuro Linguistic Programming and Transactional Analysis etc., He spent the leisure time in Mentoring, Networking, Photography and Travelling.

145

9 798895 884812